Gaining Cooperation

Some Simple Steps to Getting Customers
to do What You Want Them to do

By

Carl Van

(AUTHOR OF THE 8 CHARACTERISTICS
OF THE AWESOME EMPLOYEE)

19.95
$ USD

INTERNATIONAL INSURANCE INSTITUTE, INC.

Written by Carl van Lamsweerde.
Book cover design and layout by Ann Van
First Edition
Copyright ©2011 International Insurance Institute, Inc.
2112 Belle Chasse Hwy. #11-319, Gretna, LA 70056
T:504-393-4570 888-414-8811
www.insuranceinstitute.com

ISBN: 1456334107
ISBN-13: 9781456334109
Printed in Charleston SC

For my beautiful wife,
Ann van Lamsweerde,
who continues to inspire me
to do my very best.

Acknowledgements

Without the support of some key customers, I would never have had the time or opportunity to write this book. I'd like to take the time to thank these especially loyal customers for their extraordinary support over the last few years:

Mike Day, Tresa Edwards, Chuck Eldredge – Rural Community Insurance Services

Gerry Wilson, Rick Adam, Rich Mariani, Karen Stickel – High Point Insurance

Kristi Weathers, Phyl Turrentine, Carolyn Bolsinger, Tony Caracciolo, Judy Nuse, Judy Davis, Beth Curry, Kim Toney, Adriann Dumars, Mark Gustafson, Mary Lovelace, Browyn Davis, Scott Kotter, Mary Bullin – State Farm

Debra Hinz, Dianne Cohen, Rebecca Hughes – Macro Pro

Carla Vesper, Pat McCarthy, Paulette McGill, Lori Desch, Jackie Parish – Allstate

Andre Bourgie, Sherry Lukow, Liz Hutchinson – Aviva Canada

Ani Naccachian, Ray Naccachian – Paragon Subrogation

Brian Baker, Brad Delaney and Dick Aten – Cincinnati Insurance

Kerri Kellan – Electric Insurance

Brad Hinkle – Alliance United

Jim Strike – AAA of Missouri

Jamie Martin – Selective

Dave Williams – ZC Sterling

Jill Kilroy, Dennis Bianchi, Steve O'Dell – Horace Mann

Linda Galloway, Tom Strauss – Montana State Fund

Rodney Pilot – Pilot Catastrophe Services

Irene Bianchi, Sandi Halpert – RSA Insurance

Martha Bright, Linda Tempe – Safe Auto

Patti Van Fossen, Scott Hurias – Secura

Wendell Lambert – Texas Farm Bureau

Brian Summers – Unifund

Jim Greer – AE21

Tom Speer – Unitrin

Sharon Savageaux – Liberty Mutual

Bruce Fisher – RenRe

Special Thanks

To my daughter Amanda van Lamsweerde (soon to be Ph.D.) who keeps teaching me how the brain really works.

To my business partner and friend, Dave Vanderpan, who's sheer charisma helps keep me in business.

To my friends Leiann Dunford and Ken Sanders who helped me keep things afloat in the most difficult of times.

To my friend Sandy Masters for support and believing in me, figuratively and financially.

To my friend and family member (my wife's step father's daughter's husband – got that!) David Bryan, for backing my video project with his skillful talents

To my coworker Karla Alcerro and my niece Laura Wimsatt who helped keep my thoughts, as well as this book, organized.

Very Special Thanks

A very special thanks to my father, John Martin, who continues to support my business efforts in every way possible, and offer his invaluable guidance whenever I need it.

About the Author

Carl Van was born Carl Christian Gregory Maria Baron van Lamsweerde. He was the second son of a prominent Dutch noble and artist, Franciscus Ludovicus Aloysius Maria Baron van Lamsweerde.

After the death of Carl's father at the age of 11, his mother, Joyce, married John E. Martin. Mr. Martin was a successful business owner and investor. Mr. Martin had tremendous influence over Carl, recapping stories of coming to America with virtually nothing and building a successful business. Carl admired his new father greatly, and marveled at his generosity.

Carl had a remarkable resemblance to his father Franz, and was greatly influenced by John. His mother would often comment, "I look at Carl and I see Franz. Then he starts to talk, and out comes John".

Carl worked his way through college, taking years of night school to earn his degree in Insurance. By the time he earned his degree, Carl was already a Regional Claims Manager, and even writing and teaching several IEA courses.

With his first marriage, came his daughter Amanda Elaine Denise Baroness van Lamsweerde, who Carl continuously proclaims is a child genius.

Carl married Ann Elizabeth Wimsatt, on July 16, 1994, and together they have lived in Sacramento, CA, Nashville, TN, and now reside in New Orleans, LA. In April of 1998, Carl sold his house, cashed in his retirement, and gambled it all on the idea that insurance companies would be interested in meaningful, real-life claims training. He created International Insurance Institute, Inc. a company dedicated to the enhancement of the insurance claims industry, and now widely considered the single best claims training company in the United States and Canada.

Carl Van has dedicated his life to studying how people think and interact, and has developed classes and programs to improve the success of individuals as well business groups.

I have known Carl since we met in kindergarten, and even back then in our school days. Carl looked out for people. Obviously, Carl was honing his skills that he uses today. It only takes a few minutes in his presence to know how passionately he believes that the greatest thing a person can do in this life, is be of service to someone in need. That, he insists, is the opportunity most of us have every single day.

In this book, Carl shares his wit, wisdom, knowledge and sixth sense of dealing with people. He's a great friend and an inspiration. I hope you find this book as valuable in your world as Carl has been in mine.

-Steve Belkin, Open All Nite Entertainment.

Table of Contents

Chapter Song References

Song	Performer	Album	Written by
Sympathy for the Devil	The Rolling Stones	Beggars Banquet	Mick Jagger, Keith Richards
U Can't Touch This	M.C. Hammer	Please Hammer, Don't Hurt 'Em	Stanley Kirk Burrell, Alonzo Miller, Rick James
Help!	The Beatles	Help!	John Lennon, Paul McCartney
El Condor Pasa	Simon and Garfunkle	Bridge Over Troubled Water	Daniel Alomía Robles Jorge Milchberg, Paul Simon
Everything You Know is Wrong	Weird Al Yankovic	Bad Hair Day	Weird Al Yankovic
It's a Little Bit Me, It's a Little Bit You	The Monkeys	Monkeemania	Neil Diamond
The Ballad of the Kingsmen	Todd Snider	East Nashville Skyline	Todd Snider
The Age of Aquarius	The 5th Dimension	From Musical "Hair"	Gerome Ragni, James Rado, Galt MacDermot
Here's Where the Story Ends	The Sundays	Reading, Writing and Arithmetic	Harriet Wheeler

Allow Me to Introduce Myself

Please allow me to introduce myself; I'm a man of wealth and taste.
"Sympathy for the Devil" – Rolling Stones

Well, not really much wealth, and according to my wife, little or no taste (at least when it comes to furniture). But I do consider myself a trainer, course designer, and coach . . . not a writer. So please, forgive me if during this book, I slip in and out of my trainer mode and; instead of just commenting on what Awesome Performers do, I actually try to teach. Just be glad I don't have a flip chart.

I prefer to talk to people rather than to write to them. I love the phone and hate e-mail. This is why I have chosen to write this book in a style, as if I am talking to someone. I will refer to you, the reader, of this book without having any idea who you are or what you do. That is to simply help me convey the concepts without tuning out. It helps me if I pretend I'm talking to someone rather than writing to them.

I mention this because I wouldn't want anyone to get mad at me and say to themselves, "What is he talking about, I don't do that." Just know that when I refer to "you," I'm talking to those of you who see the need for improvement and want help.

I freely use the word "we" throughout this book, because I want you to know I consider myself an employee. No matter what project I may be working on, or any business endeavor I may be involved in, I NEVER forget that I am an employee, and never want anyone else to forget it either. After all, I am not writing this book for the upper echelon of management; I am writing it for those of us who consider ourselves employees. So I hope nobody minds that I fight to stay in the club.

Another thing you should know when reading this book, is that in most cases when I use names for customers and employees, that those are not the actual names of those employees and/or customers. They are the names of friends and family members. I decided this might increase the chance that someone might read this book if they knew their name was in it.

However, when I refer to actual Awesome Employees and use first and last name, rest assured that these people are real, and are out there right now being awesome. Some have since moved into management, and others love their jobs so much they stay right where they are.

Admission #1: I am not a researcher. You should know that I did not conduct formal research. I have no control groups to test out my theories, and no written documentation to substantiate each and every hypothesis. What I do offer is practical experience and examples to better qualify how to gain cooperation. After 30+ years in the business world, years of management and executive experience, 15+ years of monitoring phone calls, designing training programs, and facilitating over 1,000 workshops, I have a certain perspective about what one can do to gain cooperation. That is what I am relying upon, so don't expect to find me in some Management Journal. I'm not there. I'm here, trying to help.

Admission #2: I'm an Insurance guy. My background in the business world comes from the insurance claims industry, as does much of my management experience, so I will hope you forgive me if I use the insurance industry as a backdrop to illustrate my point with real-life situations. Regardless of the type of business you may be in, I am sure you will agree that the lessons learned can apply to almost anyone.

Admission #3: I'm Lazy. (Probably has something to do with Admission #1) My first book, *The 8 Characteristics* *of the Awesome Adjuster*, was quite successful in the claims world. Ever since its release, I have been bombarded with people telling me the skills, characteristics, and attitudes that make great claims people mentioned in the book are completely transferable to almost any industry. After years of people telling me that I should rewrite it with a more general outlook, I finally agreed. That book is called, *The 8 Characteristics of the Awesome Employee.*

I dedicated quite a large section of that book to gaining cooperation, and decided to give that information its own platform, and now we have <u>this</u> book. Is that lazy or what? Yes, the information is the same, the names are the same, and even the titles of the chapters are the same. Lazy!

Admission #4: I have a terrible memory. I want to tell you that <u>every</u> <u>single</u> story I tell in the book about me, things I have witnessed, things people have said to me are absolutely true!

Well, mostly true. Probably all except two...MAYBE three. Which three? I'm not telling you. You see, although I have every intention of telling the truth, or at least how I remember things, I don't intend to sit on The Daily Show or The Today Show someday trying to justify every little detail. This way, if I'm caught exaggerating, or challenged by one of my previous managers that I make fun of, I can just say, "That's one of the three."

Admission #5: I hate being sued. So, throughout this book, I am going to refer to people by name. Sometimes they're real people with their real names or real people and with fake names. Sometimes, I might even make up a fake person and a fake name.

I might be telling a story from a prior article, book, magazine, or even video presentation. I might tell the exact same story but with two different people's names. The reason for that is very simple. Sometimes I use fake names because I don't want to get sued. Would you want to get sued? No, of course you wouldn't. And neither do I. If I do make any money off of this book, I certainly don't want to spend it in legal fees defending myself against some idiot because I've used his real name in a book. So, for the most part, I will probably be using fake names.

However, there will be times when I use real people and their real names. Those times will probably be when I give you both their first and last name. So when I refer to someone by their whole name, you can be assured that these people really exist and the stories are somewhat accurate, at least to the best of my memory.

So, if you happen to read an article I wrote a number of years ago and I am telling a story and I use a different person's name, don't get your undies in a bunch. It's just what I do. I just like to use names because referring to people as "my manager," "my co-worker," "my partner," all the time can become a little monotonous. So just bear with me and come along for the ride.

CHAPTER I

Hammer Time

Stop....Hammer time!
      "U Can't Touch This" – MC Hammer

Before we can discuss the right way to be persuasive, we must rule out the wrong way to be persuasive, and that is what I lovingly refer to as "the cooperation hammer."

The Cooperation Hammer

As employees we constantly need to gain cooperation from people. Some people in their particular disciplines of their daily lives don't need to work too hard in order to gain cooperation from people. Grocery store clerks, for example, don't need to convince customers that they need to go pick out their items and bring them to him/her. They don't need to convince the customer that they need to take the items out of the basket and put them on the belt to be scanned. They don't need to convince anyone that when they ring up the total they should pay for it.

A grocery store clerk may, however, have to convince a customer that the coupons that they are using aren't the right ones. Or that just because an item is mispriced, doesn't mean the customer is entitled to get the item for that price, or a number of other things.

Many other industries, however, involve a bit of convincing. A retail clerk might need to convince a customer that they have to fill out a form in order to have a product shipped to them. A doctor's receptionist might have to convince a patient to complete a medical evaluation form in order to be seen by the doctor. There is an endless list of examples when people have to convince someone to cooperate with them.

Employees spend an incredible amount of time just negotiating for cooperation: Trying to convince a customer to fill out a form, to sign an authorization to get something repaired, or to sign a release to be seen by an ER doctor. Unfortunately, most of us go about the process exactly the opposite way that it is most effective. We pull out the cooperation hammer.

The cooperation hammer is the tool we pull out to convince someone to cooperate with us. The object is to inflict so much pain that there is no way the person can stand it so they finally do what we ask them to do.

Let's take the example where Suzanne, a retail clerk, is trying to get her customer, Mr. Wimsatt, to complete a survey form so that he can get the advertised discount he is looking for. The conversation might go like this:

Suzanne: *Mr. Wimsatt, in order for me to apply that discount, you need to complete a survey form on line.*

Mr. Wimsatt: *I'm not doing that, no way.*

Suzanne: *Well if you don't, there's no way I can give you the discount.* (Whack!)

Once again, the approach in order to gain cooperation is to pull out the cooperation hammer and start whacking away. You might ask yourself, "Why is this the wrong tool? This works." People do cooperate when we inflict pain on them. My response is, of course it works. The problem with the cooperation hammer is not that it doesn't work; the problem with it is that it works just fine.

We can inflict pain on people so they cooperate with us. However, once you gain cooperation by inflicting pain on a customer, all you have now is an angry customer who's going to try to get back at you at every turn. It's going to be why they don't cooperate with you, it's going to be why they question everything you do, it's why they're going to challenge everything that you say. Because you pushed them into doing something they didn't want to do, because you could, because you are stronger than they are. You just darn well proved it to them.

What is this cooperation hammer we love to pull out? Well, usually it is the facts. We love to hit people with the facts. We do it all the time. Do any of these sound familiar: "If you won't sign this release, we can't rent you the skis" (Whack); "If you don't give me your social security number, I can't sign into your account" (Whack); "If you won't let us inspect your property, we won't list it as a rental" (Whack).

We use force because we are stronger than they are, and we have a big cooperation hammer, which we use to whack them until they can't take the pain anymore. They finally do what we asked them to do. But, we now have a built-in enemy.

So how do we help? Start using the word.

CHAPTER 2

Help!

Help. I need somebody.
Help. Not just anybody.
Help. You know I need someone...HELP!
"Help" – The Beatles

A dividing line I have found between truly awesome performers who are customer service providers, and everybody else, is that people who make outstanding customer
service providers are people who use the word "help" a
lot. It's in their daily vocabulary.

You see, they actually believe that they are in the business of providing assistance to people. So they use the
word help a lot. Instead of saying, "Let me tell you why
we did that," they will actually say, "Let me help you understand why we do this." Instead of saying, "You are
going to have to fill out this form or else we can't pay
you," they will say, "If you can fill out the form, I can help

you by making sure you get paid." They use the word help a lot.

They don't say, "I have been assigned to handle your case," they will say, "I am going to be helping you with this matter." The word help just seems to slip out very often. And because they use the word help quite a bit, they tend to do a great job with customer service, because people tend to trust someone who is trying to help them.

Let's say you have the entire spectrum of trust. A line, with all the things you can do to make someone not trust you on one end, and all the things you can do to make someone trust you on the other end.

NO TRUST_____**TRUST**

One of the things you can do to make people not trust you, clear on the left side, is threaten them. Give someone an ultimatum, and see if they ever trust you again. Clear on the right side, to make people want to trust you, is to offer to help them. You see, most people trust someone who is trying to help them, and they don't trust someone who is trying to threaten them, hurt them, or give them an ultimatum.

Is there a difference between telling someone, "If you don't sign this form we can't pay you" and "If you do sign this form I can help make sure you get paid"? What do you think? Is there a difference between those two statements? One is a threat and an ultimatum, and the other one is an offer to help.

The funny thing about it is sometimes we actually believe we are trying to help somebody when we threaten them. We are actually thinking, "I am going to help this person understand that if they don't sign this form they won't get paid." The problem is sometimes that it comes off as a threat. So the people who tend to make the best customer service providers are people who use the word help. A lot! Because they use the word help, they get people to calm down and trust them much more than the average employee.

Usually, the cooperation hammer will work. However, most often it is not the right tool. I propose that there is another tool that can be used. The tool Awesome Employees pull out, before the cooperation hammer, is the "Why" tool. That's right, a simple question, one word, "Why."

Let me demonstrate the value of this tool. I was listening in on a conversation in a claims office (Admission #2), and the employee, let's call him Pat since Rich Farley would sue me if he knew I was using his real name (Admission #5), was trying to settle a total loss with a customer. Rich, uh, I mean Pat, had his array of facts, and including a fair market evaluation report completed by a company called CCC. It showed the value of the customer's vehicle to be about $12,500. Pat calls up the customer, and here is what I heard:

Pat: *Mr. Blasz, I have the fair market evaluation back on your car and it turns out that your car is worth $12,500. We'd like to pay you $12,500 to settle your claim.*

Mr. Blasz: *No, I really feel my car is worth $13,000.*

Pat: *Well, I have a CCC report that says it's worth $12,500. (Whack!)*

Mr. Blasz: *Well, I still feel my car is worth $13,000.*

Pat: *Mr. Blasz, you know if you don't take the $12,500, we can't pay the storage charges on your car anymore. (Whack!)*

Mr. Blasz: *Look, I understand, but I still feel my car is worth $13,000.*

Pat: *If we don't settle this today, we're not going to be able to pay for your rental car any longer either. (Whack!)*

Mr. Blasz: *Look, like I said, I really feel my car is worth $13,000.*

Pat: *Okay, but if you don't take the offer, you're still going to have to make your car payment. (Whack!)*

Of course listening to this, I knew that Pat was going to have a difficult time settling this case, which he didn't do in that conversation. So I went out to Pat after this conversation, and I said, "You know, I think if you would have changed your process just barely, you could have settled this case. See, you're trying to convince this person to give in. It's <u>much</u> easier to convince someone you're right, than it is to get them to give in if they think you are wrong."

Pat looked at me, shrugged his shoulders and said, "Ahh, he'll get tired of walking."

You know what? Pat is right, that customer will get tired of walking. In a week, he's going to call up and say, "Fine I'll take your stupid $12,500." In the meantime, he will have trashed the company's name all over the place, called up three times to make complaints, and caused a tremendous amount of time and trouble for Pat. The cooperation hammer will work, it'll work just fine. But, it will take a lot of time to inflict so much pain on the person before they finally give in, that it's a big time-waster and very big loss of customer service.

Guess what question Pat never asked the customer, not one single time? That's right, he never asked him "Why." He never said, "Why do you feel your car is worth $13,000?"

Pat never asked "Why" because he has his cooperation hammer and it works just fine. What does he care what the customer's reasons are? He's going to win this fight.

He's got his cooperation hammer, and he will whack away at this customer until the customer surrenders. And when the customer does, Pat will think to himself, "Man, am I ever a good negotiator!"

As you read this, let me ask you, are you curious why this customer wanted $13,000? Well, I certainly was. I was dying of curiosity. So you know what I did? I did something I almost never do, I called this customer and I talked to him.

I called up the customer (not really Mr. Blasz, that's just an attorney friend of mine) and I said, "Hello, my name is Carl Van and I was monitoring the phone call you were just on for quality assurance, I hope you don't mind." Of course the customer bitched at me for the next 15 minutes and said things like, "Yeah? Well, you guys suck." And I said, "Yeah, I know, but let me ask you a few questions anyway."

But after a few minutes he calmed down a little bit, and I was able to get some information out of him. By the end of the conversation I said, "Okay, thanks, I appreciate the information. Oh, and by the way, I'm just curious, why do you feel your car is worth $13,000?"

You know, the answer to that question had nothing to do with any CCC fair market evaluation report. It had nothing to do with car payments. It had nothing to do with storage charges. And it certainly had nothing to do with his staying in a rental car. The reason this customer wanted $13,000 for his car had absolutely <u>nothing</u> to do with what Pat was literally beating him to death with. Pat just didn't know it because he didn't pull out the right tool; he never asked why.

CHAPTER 3

Hammer Time
Revisited

I'd rather be a hammer than a nail
     "El Condor Pasa" – Simon and Garfunkel

STEPS TO GAINING
COOPERATION: 1. WHY?

                                2.

                                3.

Guess what he did pull out? He pulled out his cooperation
hammer and started whacking away. And in a week Pat's
going to settle this case and feel like he did his job. The
downfall is, he's taken much, and much more time than he
ever had to if he had pulled out the right tool. He could
have pulled out "Why," but he didn't.

Do you know what this customer said to me when I asked him why he wanted $13,000? He said, "Look, my brother gave me that car, and he died about six months ago. It's all I have from him. And I know someone had recently offered him $13,000 for it, and I'm not going to let you guys rip him off."

Can you imagine the feelings this customer has wrapped up in this car? Do you think there is any way this customer is going to be swayed by storage charges? Think about it. If this customer was to accept anything less than $13,000, then he would be letting an insurance company rip off his dead brother. Is this customer going to be convinced by rental charges? Is he going to give in because Pat brought up car payments? Of course he won't. Pat will never know it; because he simply never asked why. He had his cooperation hammer, and he used it.

There's an old saying and it goes like this: "When all you have is a hammer, everything looks like a nail." Perhaps from Abraham Maslow, *The Psychology of Science,* 1966. Guess what that means. It's very simple. It doesn't matter if you need a saw, it doesn't matter if you need a pair of pliers, and it certainly doesn't matter if you need sand paper. If all you have is a hammer, you're going to use it, even if it's the wrong tool. Why, because it's all you've got. And what do you do with hammers? You hit things with them.

We often times try to convince other people to do what we want by pulling out the cooperation hammer and inflicting pain on them. We don't mean it literally to cause them pain, but in effect that's what it does. By telling someone what will happen to them, if they don't do what we ask them, we are inflicting pain upon that person.

I would like to submit this. To tell someone, "Here's how this will hurt you if you don't do this" will get a different reaction than, "Here's how this will help you if you do this." These are two completely different things. They both gain cooperation, but one doesn't start a war like the other one does.

Funny thing with this "Why" tool, is that even if we ask the other person why, we often still resort to our pounding away with the cooperation hammer. Let's return to that original conversation where the employee wanted the customer to complete the on-line survey form. Here is how the call goes:

Suzanne: *Mr. Wimsatt, in order for me to apply that discount, you need to complete a survey form on line.*

Mr. Wimsatt: *I'm not doing that, no way.*

Suzanne: *Well if you don't, there's no way I can give you the discount. -* Whack!

Mr. Wimsatt: *Look, I'm not going to complete that survey.*

Suzanne: *Why not?*

Mr. Wimsatt: *Look, I got a card in the mail about a discount, but I lost it. So I called your store and they told me to come on down, that I didn't need the card. They didn't say anything about having to complete some stupid survey. Why should I run around doing your job? Now I'm the victim of some marketing ploy.*

Suzanne: *Mr. Wimsatt, it's not my job to do the survey. They probably didn't tell you because they assumed you read it on the card. If you want your discount, you're going to have to do the survey. - Whack!*

Mr. Wimsatt: *I'm not doing it.*

Suzanne: *Why not?*

Mr. Wimsatt: *I told you why!*

Suzanne: *Well if you don't, I can't give you the discount. - Whack!*

Notice a couple of things. The first thing I want you to notice is the employee finally did pull out her "Why" tool, but after annoying the customer. First she gave him a nice big whack with her cooperation hammer, before even bothering to ask why. Most of the time, we will ask the person who is not cooperating "Why," eventually. Unfortunately, it's not our first response, our first response is to give them a nice big whack with our co-operation hammers, and then if it occurs to us, we will finally ask "Why." But by that time, the process of the argument has already started.

Notice the second thing. After the employee asked Why, she went right back to using her cooperation hammer.

I'm going to make a statement now that you, the reader, may disagree with. I haven't provided you with enough evidence to convince you, but perhaps by the end of this book I will. However, I want to bring up the point now, just to lay the groundwork.

I've had the opportunity to monitor phone calls and make observations all over the U.S. and Canada, in many different situations. If you do nothing but listen to phone calls all day, you are bound to hear arguments. Based on my observations; most arguments are started by the employee, who didn't hear what the customer just said. And I mean what they just said. Most arguments could be completely avoided if both parties actually heard what the other person was saying.

Take the example above. When Suzanne finally does ask why, Mr. Wimsatt told her why, which is what Suzanne reacted to. Suzanne reacted to what she thought she heard, which is "Why should I do your job?" Unfortunately, what she didn't hear was that Mr. Wimsatt just called himself a victim. This guy used the word victim to describe himself.

Mr. Wimsatt said, "Why should I run around doing your job? Now I'm the victim of some marketing ploy." The key words were not the question about the job, which is what Suzanne heard, but the fact that this person called himself a victim.

While I was listening to this conversation, right away it was rather obvious to me this person was clearly saying why he wouldn't cooperate. He used the word victim to describe himself. What do we normally associate the word victim with? Usually, it's associated with a crime of some sort. This person is using the same word that he might use to describe himself in the event he was held up or robbed or attacked in some way. He is using the word "victim" to describe himself.

And the funny thing about it is he's perfectly justified in feeling that way. The way he sees it, he wasn't doing anything wrong. He's just coming in the store, as he was invited to do, and now he has to jump through hoops and waste more time away from work, and he's the one who's being inconvenienced. None of this is fair, and for him to feel like a victim is perfectly reasonable. The problem is the employee didn't hear that, she heard, "Why should I have to run around doing your job?"

What should have been that employee's response? Well, I could tell you that even if she had heard the person using the word victim, she likely still would have pulled out her cooperation hammer as we all would and now try to convince the person that they are wrong. We are going to try to convince them that they are wrong for the way they feel. And we are going to say something along the lines of, "Oh no, you're not a victim, you shouldn't feel that way."

Can you ever change the way someone feels by giving them a bunch of facts? It usually doesn't work, and it usually makes them feel stupid and then they dig in and then you have two issues. You are trying to change the way they feel, and they don't want to feel stupid.

Most of us do a very good job of listing a bunch of facts, figures, and reasons why someone should change the way they feel. Unfortunately, that doesn't work very well. So why do we use it? Because it's the only tool we have. We don't have any other tool, so we pull out the cooperation hammer and we start whacking away with facts and figures, trying to change the way someone feels. I gave you the first tool, which is the question why. Now I would like to give you the second tool that might actually work in changing the way someone feels.

STEPS TO GAINING
COOPERATION: 1. WHY?

                                2. ACKNOWLEDGE

                                3.

CHAPTER 4

Everything You Know is Wrong

Everything you know is wrong. Black is white, up is down and short is long.
And everything you thought was just so important... doesn't really matter anymore.
"Everything You Know is Wrong" – Weird Al Yankovic

STEPS TO GAINING
COOPERATION: 1. WHY?

                                2. ACKNOWLEDGE

                                3.

If you are a fan of the show "Seinfeld" like I am, you will remember an episode where George concludes that every single decision he made and every single approach he took in his past was wrong. Every gut instinct he had had always led him to disaster. So he incorporates a new philosophy: if every single thing that he had ever done was wrong, then the opposite must be right. And from that point forward, instead of doing what he would normally do, he does the exact opposite. Of course things work out very well for him. He gets a new girlfriend, he gets a new job, and his life becomes quite blissful (for a while).

I'm not suggesting that philosophy, but I am suggesting that in order to be persuasive, we pull out the cooperation hammer, which is the exact opposite of what we should use. Most of us tend to pull out the cooperation hammer and start whacking away when we are trying to convince someone of our point of view. In fact, we will be very detailed in pointing out why their beliefs are wrong and hitting them with our cooperation hammer so hard that they give in. Keep in mind, once again, I'm not saying this doesn't work, I'm just saying that you will have a battle on your hands that you don't need to have.

After years of listening to people trying to gain cooperation, I have developed a theory about negotiation. I call it "Carl's Theory about Negotiation." Here it is: Great negotiators never argue with reasons; they argue the facts!

Read it again and think about that just for a second. Great negotiators never argue with reasons; they argue the facts.

What are we negotiating? We are negotiating for cooperation. And when negotiating for cooperation, I have found that the very best negotiators never argue with people's reasons; they argue with facts.

You see, when you argue with someone's reasons, you are trying to prove them wrong. In fact, most of us believe that in order to convince someone we're right, we have to show them that they are wrong. It is just a natural response for us. It's a kind of "Let me show you that you are wrong so that you will see that I am right" impulse.

However (again after years of monitoring phone calls and observing employee interaction), I have come to the conclusion that you never have to prove anyone wrong; you only have to prove yourself right. Whoa...wait just a minute! That sounded pretty heavy. We HAVE to name that one. Yeah, you guessed it; "Carl's Theory about Negotiation #2." You never have to prove anyone wrong; you only have to prove yourself right. That's going in a frame and on a wall somewhere.

So, what do they do with people's reason if not argue? Well, George tried the opposite.

The opposite of hitting a customer with a cooperation hammer to get them to give in from the pain, is to simply acknowledge where they are coming from. Awesome Employees use the tool of acknowledgement to gain cooperation and save time.

Acknowledgement: The real power tool.

Yes, the cooperation hammer is a pretty good tool, and as a matter of fact in some cases it might be the right one, but what I would like to introduce is what I refer to as a power tool. A power tool does the same job as the original tool, but much more effectively and efficiently. The power tool that can change the way someone feels is Acknowledgement.

In the event you are trying to be persuasive, the first two steps are pretty clear. The first is to ask the question "Why", and the second one is to acknowledge the person's point of view.

I would like to propose a maxim. A maxim is a truth to be held. The maxim I would like to propose is this: "People will consider what you have to say; to the exact degree you demonstrate you understand their point of view." Let's call this "Carl's Cooperation Maxim" for now until somebody sues me over it.

Through the years of observing interactions, I've found this to be very true. People will consider what you have to say to the exact degree you demonstrate you understand their point of view. Let's take a look at this.

In the previous example, the employee clearly started an argument by pulling out the cooperation hammer and whacking away at this customer who didn't want to complete a survey. Watch how the tempo of the conversation changes, if the employee uses the right tool. Teresa George knew how to use this tool. Today she is a good friend and wine maker, but at one time she was one of my awesome employees. Here is how she would have handled it:

Teresa: *Mr. Wimsatt, in order for me to apply that discount, you need to complete a survey form on line.*

Mr. Wimsatt: *I'm not doing that, no way.*

Teresa: *Can I ask why?*

Mr. Wimsatt: Look, I got a card in the mail about a discount, but I lost it. So, I called your store and they told me to come on down, that I didn't need the card. They didn't say anything about having to complete some stupid survey. Why should I run around doing your job? Now, I'm the victim of some marketing ploy.

Teresa: *Mr. Wimsatt, if you don't want to complete the survey, because you are feeling like a victim right now, I can understand that. I know you can't be expected to remember every tiny detail on some card and now you were dragged into this thing that you didn't want to be in. Now you are being asked to take the time to try to deal with all this. If you feel that that's unfair, and if you feel like the victim, I completely understand that; that's very reasonable.*

Notice what Teresa did in this case. She completely reduced the person's anger by acknowledging it. Notice she did not agree with it, and notice she did not say "Yes, you are right, you are a victim." She simply acknowledged where the person was coming from. She called the customer a reasonable person. He's reasonable for the way he feels. The fact that Teresa took the time to tell this customer that he was a reasonable person for the way he feels is going to turn this person's feelings around.

Now, the more closely Teresa ties what she wants the customer to do with the customer changing the way he feels, the more likely he will do it. Let me repeat, the more closely Teresa ties what she wants the customer to do, to the customer changing his feelings, the more likely the customer is to do it. You will see in the next chapter how Teresa uses this tool and returns the conversation to the facts.

CHAPTER 5

Don't Want to Fight

I don't want to fight. I'm a little bit wrong, you're a little bit right
You know that it's true. It's a little bit me; it's a little bit you.
"A Little Bit Me, A Little Bit You" – The Monkeys

STEPS TO GAINING
COOPERATION: 1. WHY?

                                2. ACKNOWLEDGE

                                3. FACTS

Teresa: *Mr. Wimsatt, if you don't want to complete the*
           survey, because you are feeling like a victim right
           now, I can understand that. I know you can't be
           expected to remember every tiny detail on some
           card and now you were dragged into this thing that
           you didn't want to be in. Now you are being asked
           to take the time to try to deal with all this. If you

feel that that's unfair, and if you feel like the victim, I completely understand that; that's very reasonable.

I'll tell you what though. If you are able to complete the survey right here at the customer service stand, some good things will happen. Number one, you won't have to come back another time. Number two, you'll be able to voice your concern about the requirement to complete the survey. And number three, by the time you finish, I will have all your transactions completed so you won't have to wait. And when we're all done, perhaps you won't have to feel like a victim anymore, because that's a lousy way to feel and I'd like to help. Would you be willing complete the survey so that I can help you?

Notice how Teresa in this case, ties in this person changing the way he feels to what she wants him to do. Once the customer does what Teresa wants him to do, he won't have to feel like a victim anymore. Teresa actually heard what the person said about feeling like a victim and used it to her advantage.

The idea of acknowledgement is extremely important. The best communicators I know use it. Rather than trying to convince someone they're wrong, it's much easier to convince them you understand where they are coming from. Remember our maxim: people will consider what you have to say to the exact degree you demonstrate you understand their point of view.

Here's a real life example: I was in Cincinnati, Ohio, one time to teach a class, when I got a call from a friend. He called me up and asked if I could help him find a hotel room because he couldn't find one anywhere in Cincinnati. He was about to get on a plane to come out that night to teach a class the next day. He didn't have time right then, so he asked for my help. I told him I would try to help him out.

After we hung up, I dialed the 800 number right on the phone of the hotel where I was staying (don't sue me, Fairfield Inn). I told the operator at the 800 number that I needed a room that night because a friend of mine was coming into town. That operator responded by saying, "Oh, no problem, we've got plenty of rooms, we're not even one-third booked. Just bring the person in tonight and they'll be sure to get a room. You don't need to make a reservation."

With that, I contacted my friend and left him a message saying, "Don't worry; we've got plenty of room at my hotel." At the time, I kind of wondered why I was able to get a room so easily when he had so much trouble, but I went off to teach my class, and I forgot about it.

After my class, I went to the airport and I picked him up and we went back to the hotel. We both walked right up to the counter and were met by Bart. I said to Bart, "Yes, hello, this is a friend of mine who needs a room for tonight and I called earlier and they said you had plenty of rooms."

Bart looked at his screen for a minute or two, shook his head and said, "You know, we're completely booked."

Obviously, I was annoyed and I responded, "No, no, no, I called the 800 number this morning and they said you had plenty of rooms." Bart's response was, "Sir, we have no rooms, we're completely booked."

Getting angry, I said, "Look, you don't understand, this puts me in a very bad situation. I've got my friend here who I told I would get a room. Now because I told him I could get him a room, he didn't go look for himself when he could have found a room in the meantime. Now, we are both standing here and he doesn't have a room, and I feel responsible. I feel caught in the middle."

Bart takes the terminal, turns it around and points to the screen, and says, "Sir, we have no more rooms!" He said this to me like he was calling me an idiot. "Look at the absolute truth, look at the undisputed evidence that there are no rooms, you idiot," is what I felt like he was trying to tell me.

All this did was infuriate me, so I said "Look, let me talk to a manager, I want to talk to a manager right now!" And he said, "Okay," walked a few steps away, and said, "Hey, Angie, THIS GUY wants to talk to you."

Now, I know the words "this guy" is code for something. It probably starts with an A, but, hey, that's just a random guess. So when he said, "this guy wants to talk to you," I already knew I was being set up for an argument.

The next thing I know, Angie walks over to us both and says, "Yes, may I help you?" And I said, "Yes, this is my friend. I called the 800 number this morning and asked to make a reservation. They told me they had plenty of rooms, and there would be no problem. Now I've picked him up at the airport and we are standing here and we are being told you have no rooms. I feel bad for my friend because now he is out of a room. That's just not right! So what's up?"

Angie pauses for a moment while she looks at the screen, and replies, *"Oh, Mr. Van. I'm so sorry. I'm sorry for the difficult situation you've been put in. I see by looking at our screen that we really don't have any rooms; the person you were talking to at the 800 number must have been looking at the wrong screen, because we have been booked for over a week. There is a huge convention in town, which is probably why your friend couldn't find a room before. I'm sorry for your inconvenience. I understand the difficulty you are going through, and I understand the position you are in, especially given the promise you made to your friend. Believe me, if we had a room right now, I would give it to you. I really would. The truth is, I just don't have a room to actually give to you. I would if I could, I just can't. Can I help you find a room somewhere else?"*

Now let me ask, of these two people who both told me "no," who was more believable? Bart, who threw the facts in my face with the screen being the reason I should believe him? Or Angie, who said she was sorry and understood where I was coming from?

Probably Angie seemed much more credible because she understood where I was coming from. She said she understood the difficult situation I was in, and if she had a room, she'd give it to me. That seemed believable to me. I believed they actually were full because she understood where I was coming from, and she was able to relate that to me.

And notice how she tactfully got back to the facts. She didn't beat me to death with the facts, but she got me to consider the facts by acknowledging my point of view.

If she had just said something along the lines of, "Yeah, I'm really sorry, there's nothing I can do," that would not have seemed as believable. The statement "I want to help you, and I would if I could, I just can't," is much more powerful than "I won't help you because I don't have to."

The idea here is to use acknowledgement as a way to get someone to believe what you are about to say. What are you acknowledging? You're acknowledging that the other person is a reasonable person for their beliefs or for their circumstance. You are not saying you agree with them, you are not saying they are right, you're simply saying that you understand where they are coming from. They are reasonable for their beliefs.

Let's apply these steps to another situation. Sarah Holton is great at this. Sarah is an assistant Vice President at one of the world's largest international insurance companies. But once upon a time she worked for me. Here is how she would handle a situation like this.

Sarah: *Mr. Dudenhofer, in order to get your medical bills, you're going to need to fill out this form.*

Mr. Dudenhofer: *I don't want to do that.*

Sarah: *Oh, can I ask why?*

Mr. Dudenhofer: *Yeah, because I was told I wouldn't have to sign anything.*

Now at this point, the vast majority of people would say, "Who told you that?" That is because we are just dying to prove this person wrong. Sarah knows it doesn't matter who said it, or even what was really said. Sarah knows that most of the time, people's reasons for not cooperating has nothing to do with the issue at hand. She knows that great negotiators never argue with reasons, they argue the facts. So, here is what Sarah says:

Sarah: *Mr. Dudenhofer, if you don't want to fill out this Medical Authorization because you were told you wouldn't have to sign anything, I understand that, that's reasonable. Who ever told you that was mistaken, and I am very sorry about that. I don't know why you were told that. Maybe they were just trying to reassure you nothing would happen without your permission, I really don't know. The truth is; I'd like you to fill out this form so I can get your medical bills paid. If you can fill out this form and return it to me, I will do everything I can to make sure I get everything I need to process your claim. But again, I do understand that you were given the wrong information and I am sorry. Would you be willing to fill out these forms so I can help you?*

Did that sound better? Is it possible that this customer might be a little bit more cooperative right now? This customer is not going to be Mr. Sunshine.

He's not going to sit there and say, "Oh boy, am I glad I got the wrong information now, thank you!" But you know what? He's a little more satisfied; he's a little calmer. He has been treated with respect and most importantly, his feelings have been acknowledged as reasonable.

He is much more open to change than he would have been if Sarah had argued with him. And at the very least, even if he stays irritated, at least he won't be irritated at Sarah. And he'll probably cooperate with her and just be irritated at somebody else.

Knowing Sarah, she might have even added, "If you know who you spoke to, I can let them know that whatever they did tell you, it might have been confusing, so we don't confuse anybody else in the future."

Can it sometimes impress a customer that you will go out of your way to solve a problem? Even if they got caught in it this time, the fact that you're willing to go out of your way to solve it for the next time, can be very impressive. But the overall tool of acknowledging where someone is coming from is a very high-powered tool and one that Awesome Employees have at their disposal at all times.

CHAPTER 6

Not Some Monster

Marilyn Manson's real name isn't even Marilyn Manson.
He's a skinny long haired public high school kid from Florida,
Not some monster from out of this world.
    "The Ballad of the Kingsmen" – Todd Snider

Uncooperative people are not monsters. They are not the enemy. Sometimes they just need some help seeing the light.

One of my favorite cartoons is from Non Sequitur. It shows a guy with a sign saying, "The facts as they are." He's facing another guy with a sign that says, "The truth as I see it" and the line underneath reads "The irresistible force meets the immovable object."

Normally, we are "the facts as they are." The uncooperative person is the "truth as I see it" person. If we get in a fight, who will win? Well, usually we will win. We have the hammer. We have the facts. We can usually pound this person into submission. But that's not the point. The point is, maybe we can get this person to see the facts as they are, and maybe he will join us. After all, it's their cooperation we are after, not to win a fight.

Let's see if we can go through some more examples of gaining cooperation using the WHY – ACKNOWLEDGE - FACTS model. No wait! We'd better name it; how about "Big Daddy's 3 Step Cooperation Model." Yeah, perfect. Big Daddy is what my niece's son calls me, and what I expect all of my grandkids will be calling me. So, as a tribute to them, let's go through some more examples of gaining cooperation using Big Daddy's 3 Step Cooperation model.

In all of these examples, you will see three versions. The first is where we don't even ask the person "Why." The second where we ask the person "Why," but then try to prove the person wrong. And the third, where we ask Why, Acknowledge their reasons, and get back to the Facts.

Jo and R.K

Jo works at an agency to help elderly people get paid for their medical expenses. R.K. is a really old customer who has signed up for assistance. Somewhere in their initial conversation, Jo realizes that R.K. does not want to cooperate.

Version 1

Jo: Okay, all I need you to do now is fill out the medical authorization form we sent you, sign it, and send it back to me so I can get busy getting your medical bills together and requesting payment.

R.K.   I'm not doing that.

Jo: You don't want to fill it out or sign it?

R.K.   Both

Jo: Then we can't get your bills paid. -Whack!

That is pretty much how most conversations would go.

Version 2

Jo: Okay, all I need you to do now is fill out the medical authorization form we sent you, sign it, and send it back to me so I can get busy getting your medical bills together and requesting payment.

R.K.   I'm not doing that.

Jo: You don't want to fill it out or sign it?

R.K.   Both

Jo: Can you tell me why?

R.K.   *Sure. Because I talked to my neighbor, and he's in his second year of law school, and he said, "Don't sign anything."*

Jo: *Well, what does your neighbor know about processing medical bills?*

Notice how Jo jumps to try to prove R.K. wrong? It's natural for us to want to show someone they are wrong. But if Jo tries this, she will fail. You see, if she attacks the neighbor in any way, she will automatically lose credibility, because her customer already trusts his neighbor much more than he trusts Jo. Also keep in mind; if Jo says anything to disparage the neighbor, she isn't really even attacking the neighbor. Guess who she is really attacking? She is really attacking R.K. for relying on his neighbor. She is literally trying to get the customer to admit listening to his neighbor was dumb before he will change his mind.

Jo should remember three important things:

1. People will consider what you have to say; to the exact degree you demonstrate you understand their point of view.

2. Great negotiators never argue with reasons; they argue the facts.

3. You never have to prove anyone wrong; you only have to prove yourself right.

Version 3

Jo: *Okay, all I need you to do now is fill out the medical authorization form we sent you, sign it, and send it back to me so I can get busy getting your medical bills together and requesting payment.*

R.K.   *I'm not doing that.*

Jo: *You don't want to fill it out or sign it?*

R.K.   *Both*

Jo: *Can you tell me why?*

R.K.   *Sure. Because I talked to my neighbor, and he's in his second year of law school, and he said, "Don't sign anything."*

Jo: *R.K., if you talked to your neighbor, and he is someone you trust and you respect his opinion, and he told you not to sign anything, then I can understand why you wouldn't want to sign the form. That's reasonable; that makes sense. This form, allows us to get your medical bills so we CAN get you paid. That is the purpose of this form. If you'll sign the form, I'll get busy gathering your bills and make sure they all get paid. Would you sign the form so I can help you?*

Now, maybe R.K. will sign the form, and maybe he won't. But my guess is he is much more likely to cooperate with someone who understands his point by acknowledging his reasons than someone who whacks him with the cooperation hammer.

Kim and Lou

Kim is a medical assistant for a highly respected dermatologist. Her job is to create a medical history for the new patients for her boss. Lou is a new patient of the good doctor and after having just set an appointment with the office was transferred to Kim, so that Kim could complete the history review. Kim is a busy person who doesn't have time for a lot of nonsense.

Version I

Kim: *Okay sir, what I am going to need to do is create a complete medical history on you. Sir, can you give me a detailed description of any medical operations you have had in the past?*

Lou: *Well, I'd really rather not get into that.*

Kim: *You don't want to answer the question?*

Lou: *No, not really.*

Kim: *Well, then the doctor can't see you. -Whack!*

Again, that is pretty much how most conversations would go. Lou would both give in and feel like he got beaten up, or he'll hang up and go to another doctor.

Version 2

Kim: Okay sir, what I am going to need to do is create a complete medical history on you. Sir, can you give me a detailed description on any medical operations you have had in the past?

Lou: Well, I'd really rather not get into that.

Kim: You don't want to answer the question?

Lou: No, not really.

Kim: Would you be able to tell me why?

Lou: Well, yeah, you see I had kind of an embarrassing operation a few years ago and I would really rather not let that information out.

Kim: Okay, but we have to have the information.

Lou: Well, like I said, it's kind of an embarrassing operation. It's kind of a delicate matter so I'd really rather not discuss it.

Kim: Maybe so, but we still need the information. It's the rule for this office that we get a complete history and we can't make an exception for you or else we would have to make an exception for everybody.

Lou: Like I said, it's just something I'd really rather not talk about.

Kim: *You're going to have to or else you can't see the doctor. Do you want to see the doctor or not?*

Lou: *Well, yes of course.*

Kim: *Then you're going to have to supply me with the information.*

Lou: *Alright, alright, fine!*

Notice how Kim jumped right into arguing with Lou's reasons. Kim should remember three important things:

1. People will consider what you have to say; to the exact degree you demonstrate you understand their point of view.

2. Great negotiators never argue with reasons; they argue the facts.

3. You never have to prove anyone wrong; you only have to prove yourself right.

Version 3

Kim: *Okay sir, what I am going to need to do is create a complete medical history on you. Sir, can you give me a detailed description on any medical operations you have had in the past?*

Lou: *Well, I'd really rather not get into that.*

Kim: *You don't want to answer the question?*

Lou: *No, not really.*

Kim: *Would you be able to tell me why?*

Lou: *Well, yeah, you see I had kind of an embarrassing operation a few years ago and I would really rather not let that information out.*

Kim: *You know what Lou, if you had an embarrassing operation a couple years ago and you would rather not go over that information now because that's a delicate subject for you, I certainly understand that. Of course, you are entitled to your privacy, and of course I understand that you don't want to be embarrassed. That's certainly reasonable.*

I just want to let you know that my goal is not to embarrass you. My goal is to do a complete medical history on you so that we can provide you with the very best of care. First of all, I probably won't have to get into any specific details about the operation. But even if I do, I want to let you know that I am going to treat this professionally because you are entitled to that as our patient.

So will Lou cooperate now? Well, he may or may not. But once again, I believe that he is more likely to cooperate with someone who shows him the respect of considering his point of view.

Mike and Rhonda

Mike works at a department store in the customer service area. His main job is to deal with people who want to get a refund for a product that did not meet their expectations or did not work properly. Rhonda is a recent customer who has brought in an item to return.

Version 1

Mike: *Okay, Rhonda, in order to process this return, all I need to do is get a statement from you on what was wrong with the product or how it didn't meet your expectations.*

Rhonda: *I don't want to give you that.*

Mike: *You don't want to give me any information on why you're returning the product?*

Rhonda: *No.*

Mike: *Well, then we can't take it back. -Whack!*

This is a pretty common reaction.

Version 2

Mike: *Okay, Rhonda, in order to process this return, all I need to do is get a statement from you on what was wrong with the product or how it didn't meet your expectations.*

Rhonda: *I don't want to give you that.*

Mike: *Well, why not?*

Rhonda: *Because, you will just use it against me.*

Mike: *Why would I use that against you? That doesn't make any sense.*

My advice again, is that Mike should remember three important things:

1. People will consider what you have to say; to the exact degree you demonstrate you understand their point of view.

2. Great negotiators never argue with reasons; they argue the facts.

3. You never have to prove anyone wrong; you only have to prove yourself right.

Version 3

Mike: *Okay, Rhonda, in order to process this return, all I need to do is get a statement from you on what was wrong with the product or how it didn't meet your expectations.*

Rhonda: *I don't want to give you that.*

Mike: *Well, why not?*

Rhonda: *Because, you will just use it against me.*

Mike: *You know, Rhonda, if you don't want to give me a statement about the product and why you're returning it; because you are concerned that I am going to use it against you, then I can certainly understand why you don't want to give me a statement. That makes sense.*

I just want to let you know that the purpose of the statement is not to use the information against you. In fact, the reason I need the statement is to document the file to be sure that you do get a full refund and that you do get everything that you are entitled to. If you'll give me a statement of facts, I will be able to process your return and you can be on your way.

Once again, in this last version, did you see how Mike took the time to acknowledge the reasons and skillfully return to the facts at hand?

Another problem I see is employees not recognizing when the time to fight is over; when the battle has already been won. The ability to recognize when the time to fight is over is just as important as winning the fight. Let's take a look at that next.

CHAPTER 7

Trust Abounding

Harmony and understanding, sympathy and trust abounding.
No more falsehoods or derisions.
Golden living dreams of visions.
Mystic crystal revelation and the mind's true liberation.
    "The Age of Aquarius" – The Fifth Dimension (Hair)

Recognizing a gift when you get it

Imagine a conversation between a department store clerk, Lhani and a customer, Jennifer.

Jennifer: *Yes, I'd like to return this for a refund, please.*

Lhani: *Well, I can return it for you, but since it was on sale for the past week, I can only refund the sale price.*

Jennifer: *That's not fair, I paid more for this just a month ago, and it's not doing what I want it to do.*

Lhani: *I understand that. It's just that I can only refund the lowest price that we had for it in the last six months, that's our store policy. Unless you have the actual receipt for the purchase, that's our policy.*

Jennifer: *No, I don't have the receipt, but I bought it a month ago for more than its sale price.*

Lhani: *I'm sorry. Our store policy is that we can only refund the amount of money that the item has been sold for. And since we don't know what that is, I have to refund just the lowest price.*

Jennifer: *That's a rip off!*

Lhani: *It's only fair because some people might come in and buy it at a lower price and then want a full refund.*

Jennifer: *I would never do anything like that!*

Lhani: *I'm not saying you would, but some people would. So that's why we do it.*

Jennifer: *I still think that's a rip off!*

Lhani: *Not really. This is what we have to do, because there's just no way of knowing what you actually paid for it. We could easily get ripped off by some people, and we are just trying to protect ourselves. That makes sense doesn't it?*

Jennifer: *It doesn't make sense to me, because now I'm going to be out $45!*

Lhani: *Well, you did use it for a month, didn't you?*

Jennifer: (getting upset) *Yes, but it didn't work right, so what good does it do me?*

Lhani: *At least you got some use out of it. That should make you feel better about losing the $45.*

Jennifer: (Getting angrier) *It doesn't make me feel better at all. All I feel is that not only have I lost $45, I've wasted my time using a product that doesn't work!*

You can see that this conversation is only going to get worse. The reason it's going to get worse is because the clerk didn't realize she already had the battle won a long time ago. Remember back when the customer said, "What a rip off!" Most people would have interpreted that as a snide comment, but the Awesome Employee recognizes that as the gift it is. Do you know what that person is saying, when they say, "What a rip off!" Think about it just for one second, what are they really saying?

Believe it or not, what this person just said is ... "I believe you." That's right. What this person just said is that they believe you. They're not happy about it, which is why they make the comment that it is a rip off, but nevertheless they do believe what you are telling them. There's no way for them to conclude that it's a rip off, unless they believe you first. If they didn't believe you, they'd keep arguing with you about whether or not it's really going to happen.

At this point, the Awesome Employee recognizes that they have convinced the person and stops all fighting. Fighting is not necessary. You don't need to inflict more pain on this person. You don't need to start an argument; this person already believes you. All you have to do from this point is empathize. You have to recognize gifts when you get them. And believe it or not, this snide comment is a gift. Take it for what it is.

Imagine the conversation going slightly differently. Let's put in Amanda. You see, although Amanda is working as a clerk in a store, she's also working toward her Ph.D. in Psychology. Here's how she handles it.

Jennifer: *Yes, I'd like to return this for a refund please.*

Amanda: *Well, I can return it for you, but since it was on sale last week, I can only refund it for the sale price.*

Jennifer: *That's not fair, I paid more for this just a month ago, and it's not doing what I want it to do.*

Amanda: *I understand that. It's just that I can only refund the lowest price that we had for it in the last six* months, that's our store policy. Unless you have the actual receipt for the purchase, that's our policy.

Jennifer: No, I don't have the receipt but, I bought it a couple of months ago for more than its sale price.

Amanda: I'm sorry. Our store policy is that we can only refund the amount of money that the item has been sold for. And since we don't know what that is, I have to refund just the lowest price.

Jennifer: That's a rip off!

Amanda: (New approach) Madam, I can understand how you feel. If it seems like a rip off I can understand that, because you are out $45. I am sorry about that. I can refund this to you in cash, or we can apply the credit to your card.

Jennifer: No, I'd rather have it in cash.

Amanda: Okay, here you go, here's your refund. Again I am sorry about the problem. And thank you for shopping with us.

Jennifer: Fine, whatever.

What's important to understand is that this customer is not going to be thrilled. She's not happy that she lost $45, but at the very least, we don't have a clerk picking a fight with a customer. Believe it or not, because this person got treated with respect, they just may be back even though they didn't get what they wanted, and that's one of the important things to understand about customer service. We want them back!

Here's Where the Story Ends

It's that little souvenir, of a colorful year, which makes me
smile inside.
Surprise, surprise, surprise, surprise, surprise.
Here's where the story ends.
    "Here's Where the Story Ends" – The Sundays

Awesome Employees have great interpersonal skills that allow them to gain cooperation from customers by focusing on how to help the customer instead of hitting them with the cooperation hammer. They know how to avoid arguments by listening to what the customer has to say and responding to the issue. They know their credibility comes from understanding the customer's point of view, not from the facts.

- Great negotiators never argue with reasons; they argue the facts!

- You never have to prove anyone wrong; you only have to prove yourself right.

- People will consider what you have to say; to the exact degree you demonstrate you understand their point of view.

Professional Speaking Services

Carl Van is a professional national speaker having delivered presentations throughout the U.S., Canada, Newfoundland and the U.K.

His presentation style is upbeat, fast paced and always generates audience participation. He has received numerous recognitions throughout the years, including Most Dynamic Speaker at the national ACE conference.

Mr. Van is qualified to speak on virtually any subject regarding employee performance and customer interaction. Just a few of his Guest Speaking titles include:

General

- Awesome Customer Service: You're Good. You Can Get Better
- How to Avoid Losing Customers
- The Customer Service Standards: 5 Things to Never Forget

- Practical Negotiations: Stop Arguing and Start Agreeing
- Real Life Time Management
- Stress Management: Give Yourself a Break Before You Die
- Improving your Attitude and Initiative
- Getting People's Cooperation – A Few Easy Steps
- What Customers Hate – And Why We Do It
- If You Can't Say it Simply and Clearly, Then You Don't Know What You're Talking About: Some Business Writing Basics
- Empathy: The Power Tool of Customer Service
- Why Are They Calling Me? Things to do to Reduce Nuisance Calls
- Let Me Do My Job: Simple Steps to get People to be Patient and Let You Do Your Job
- Trust Me: Effective Ways to Gain Credibility
- Saying No: The Right Way (and easy way), or The Wrong Way (the hard way)
- Listening Skills: How to Avoid Missing the Point
- Teamwork: Ways to Reduce the Work Created by Individualism

Management

- Handling Your Difficult Employees (Without Threats and Violence)
- Teaching and Coaching for Supervisors and Managers
- Initiative: How to Develop it in Your Staff

- Stop Wasting Your Time – Practical Time Management for Managers
- Effective Delegation: Why People Hate It When You Delegate, and How to Change That
- Managing Change
- Interviewing and Hiring Exceptional Performers
- Motivating Your Team
- How to Make Sure Your Employees get the Most out of Training
- Inspiring Employees to Improve Themselves

For a free DVD, please visit www.CarlVan.org or call 504-393-4570

In-Person Training Services

Carl Van is President & CEO of an international training company that delivers high quality training directly to customers at their locations. He is the author of over 75 technical and soft skill courses that have been delivered to over 100,000 employees throughout the U.S, Canada, Newfoundland and the U.K.

Just of few titles of his programs include:

Employee Soft-Skill

- Real-Life Time Management for Employees
- The 8 Characteristics of the Awesome Employee
- Negotiation Training
- Conflict Resolution
- Awesome Customer Service
- Managing the Telephone
- Attitude & Initiative Training for the Employee
- Empathy & Listening Skills
- Employee Organization – Managing the Desk

- Prepare for Promotion – Employee Leadership Training
- Teamwork Basics – No Employee is an Island
- Interpersonal Skills – Improving Team Member Relations
- Effective Recorded Statements
- Business Writing Skills for Employees
- Beating Anxiety and Dealing with Anger – Help for the New Employee

Manager Soft-Skill

- Time Management for Supervisors and Managers
- Coaching and Teaching for Supervisors and Managers
- Keys to Effective Presentations
- Teaching Your Employees the 8 Characteristics of Awesome Employees
- Motivating Your Team
- Handling Difficult Employees
- The New Supervisor
- Interviewing and Hiring Exceptional Performers
- Delegation Training for Supervisors and Managers
- Managing Change
- Team Training
- Leadership Skills for Supervisors and Managers
- Preparing Effective Performance Appraisals
- Managing the Highly Technical Employee

For more information and a free catalog of courses, please visit www.InsuranceInstitute.com or call 504-393-4570

On-Line Training Services

Carl Van is President and owner of an on-line website delivering high quality training through streaming video that employees can access anywhere in the world.

He is also available to write, direct and present training courses specific to an individual company or industry. He wrote and presented a customer service course on DVD for a national company which was rolled out to all 18,000 line employees.

He is designer, author and presenter of four on-line video training courses:

- Exceptional Claims Customer Service
- Negotiation Skills for the Claims Professional
- Real-Life Time Management for Claims
- Critical Thinking for Claims

For more information, visit www.ClaimsEducationOnLine. com

EDUCATIONAL ARTICLES BY CARL VAN

Carl Van is owner and publisher of his own educational magazine, and is the author of numerous articles that have appears in various periodicals.

Just a sample of articles written by Carl Van

Van, Carl. "5th Annual Claims Education Conference Earns Superbowl Status." Claims Education Magazine. Summer 2010: Pg. 1.

Van, Carl. "While Others Wait, Bold Companies Invest in Training." Subrogator. Winter 2010: Pg. 102.

Van, Carl. "While Others Wait, Bold Companies Invest in Training Part III." Claims Education Magazine. Spring 2010: Pg. 1.

Van, Carl. "While Others Wait, Bold Companies Invest in Training Part II." Claims Education Magazine. December 2009- Vol. 6, No. 6: Pg. 1.

Van, Carl. "While Others Wait, Some Invest in Training." Claims Education Magazine. October/November 2009- Vol. 6, No. 5: Pg. 3

Van, Carl. "Tips on Taking Statements & Information Gathering." Claims Education Magazine. October/November 2009- Vol. 6, No. 5: Pg. 1.

Van, Carl. "Placing the Bets." Claims Education Magazine. March/April 2009- Vol. 6, No. 2: Pg. 1.

Van, Carl. "Lesson in Customer Service & Attitude." Claims Education Magazine. January/February 2009- Vol. 6, No. 1: Pg. 1.

Van, Carl. "Saying It the Right Way." Claims Education Magazine. Fall 2008- Vol. 5, No. 4: Pg. 8.

Van, Carl. "Critical Thinking Part Three." Claims Education Magazine. Summer 2008- Vol. 5, No. 3: Pg. 4.

Van, Carl. "Critical Thinking Part Two." Claims Education Magazine. Spring 2008- Vol. 5, No. 2: Pg. 4.

Van, Carl. "Critical Thinking Part One." Claims Education Magazine. Winter 2008- Vol. 5, No. 1: Pg. 4.

Van, Carl. "Desire for Excellence." Claims Education Magazine. Fall 2007- Vol. 4, No. 4: Pg. 14.

Van, Carl. "Building a Claim Team." Claims. October 2005.

Van, Carl. "In Search of Initiative." Claims. September 2005.

Van, Carl. "A Velvet Hammer Can Expedite Negotiations." Claims Education Magazine. Summer 2005- Vol. I, No. I: Pg. 10.

Van, Carl. "Claims Management: Desire for Excellence." Claims. July 2005.

Van, Carl. "Empathizing with Customers." Claims. June 2005.

Van, Carl. "Never Stop Learning." Claims. May 2005.

Van, Carl. "Interpersonal Skills: Avoid the Hammer." Claims. April 2005.

Van, Carl. "Secrets of Successful Time Management." Claims. March 2005.

Van, Carl. "Attitude." Claims Magazine. February 2005: Pg. 10.

Van, Carl. "Tend to Your Garden: A Vision of Claims Education." Claims. February 2003: Pg. 34.

Van, Carl. "Adjusters: How not to Drive Away Clients." National Underwriter. September 24, 2001.

Van, Carl & Sue Tarrach. "The 8 Characteristics of Awesome Adjusters." Claims. December 1996.

Carl Van is available for consulting, training and guest speaking appearances. To contact Mr. Van, call 504-393-4570 or visit:

www.facebook.com/CarlVanSpeaker

ARTICLES FEATURING CARL VAN

Mr. Van has been the subject of numerous articles outlining his services and educational philosophy. A few are:

Gilkey, Eric. "Strategies for Gaining Cooperation." IASIU. Monday, September 13, 2010: Pg. 4.

Henry, Susan, and Mary Anne Medina. "Evaluating Adjuster Performance." Claims. August 2010: Pg. 36.

"Permission to Say, 'I'm Sorry.'" Canadian Underwriter. September 1, 2008.

Aznoff, Dan. "Fair Oaks Students Take Speaker's Advice to Heart for Positive Attitude." The Sacramento Bee. April 12, 2007: City Section, Pg. G5.

Friedman, Sam. "WC Claimants 'Not the Enemy,' Trainer says." National Underwriter. September 24, 2001.

Prochaska, Paul. "Awesome Adjusting Revisited: A Return to Customer Service." Claims. February, 2000.

Hays, Daniel. "Being Kinder and Gentler Pays Off: Insurance Claims is a Customer Service Business." Claims. December 2000: Pg. 56.

Carl Van is available for consulting, training and guest speaking appearances. Follow Carl Van on Twitter at www.twitter.com/CarlVanSpeaker

BOOKS BY CARL VAN

Van, Carl. "The 8 Characteristics of the Awesome Adjuster." Published by Arthur Hardy Enterprises, Inc., ISBN 0-930892-66-6 (Metaire, LA) Copyright © 2005

Van, Carl. "The 8 Characteristics of the Awesome Employee". To be published in 2011.

Van, Carl. "Gaining Cooperation: Some Simple Steps to Getting Customers to do What You Want Them to do". Published by **INTERNATIONAL INSURANCE INSTITUTE, INC.** Copyright © 2011

Carl Van is available for consulting, training and guest speaking appearances. To contact Mr. Van, call 504-393-4570 or visit:

www.CarlVan.org
www.InsuranceInstitute.com
www.ClaimsEducationOnLine.com
www.ClaimsEducationMagazine.com
www.ClaimsEducationConference.com
www.ClaimsSkillsAcademy.com
www.facebook.com/CarlVanSpeaker
http://twitter.com/carlvanspeaker
www.Linkedin.com/CarlVan

Made in the USA
Charleston, SC
22 June 2014